EASY POP MELODIES
FOR ALTO SAX

ISBN 978-1-4803-8430-9

HAL•LEONARD®
CORPORATION

7777 W. BLUEMOUND RD. P.O. BOX 13819 MILWAUKEE, WI 53213

For all works contained herein:
Unauthorized copying, arranging, adapting, recording, Internet posting, public performance,
or other distribution of the printed or recorded music in this publication is an infringement of copyright.
Infringers are liable under the law.

Visit Hal Leonard Online at
www.halleonard.com

ALL MY LOVING

ALTO SAX

Words and Music by JOHN LENNON
and PAUL McCARTNEY

Copyright © 1963, 1964 Sony/ATV Music Publishing LLC
Copyright Renewed
All Rights Administered by Sony/ATV Music Publishing LLC, 8 Music Square West, Nashville, TN 37203
International Copyright Secured   All Rights Reserved

BEAUTY AND THE BEAST

from Walt Disney's BEAUTY AND THE BEAST

ALTO SAX

Lyrics by HOWARD ASHMAN
Music by ALAN MENKEN

© 1991 Walt Disney Music Company and Wonderland Music Company, Inc.
All Rights Reserved   Used by Permission

BLOWIN' IN THE WIND

ALTO SAX

Words and Music by
BOB DYLAN

Copyright © 1962 Warner Bros. Inc.
Copyright Renewed 1990 Special Rider Music
International Copyright Secured   All Rights Reserved
Reprinted by Permission of Music Sales Corporation

CAN YOU FEEL THE LOVE TONIGHT

from Walt Disney Pictures' THE LION KING

ALTO SAX

Music by ELTON JOHN
Lyrics by TIM RICE

© 1994 Wonderland Music Company, Inc.
All Rights Reserved   Used by Permission

CAN'T HELP FALLING IN LOVE

ALTO SAX

Words and Music by GEORGE DAVID WEISS,
HUGO PERETTI and LUIGI CREATORE

Copyright © 1961; Renewed 1989 Gladys Music (ASCAP)
All Rights in the U.S. Administered by Imagem Sounds
International Copyright Secured   All Rights Reserved

CLOCKS

ALTO SAX

Words and Music by GUY BERRYMAN,
JON BUCKLAND, WILL CHAMPION
and CHRIS MARTIN

Copyright © 2002 by Universal Music Publishing MGB Ltd.
All Rights in the United States Administered by Universal Music - MGB Songs
International Copyright Secured   All Rights Reserved

DAYDREAM BELIEVER

ALTO SAX

Words and Music by
JOHN STEWART

© 1967 (Renewed 1995) SCREEN GEMS-EMI MUSIC INC.
All Rights Reserved   International Copyright Secured   Used by Permission

DON'T KNOW WHY

ALTO SAX

Words and Music by
JESSE HARRIS

Copyright © 2002 Sony/ATV Music Publishing LLC and Beanly Songs
All Rights Administered by Sony/ATV Music Publishing LLC, 8 Music Square West, Nashville, TN 37203
International Copyright Secured   All Rights Reserved

DON'T STOP BELIEVIN'

ALTO SAX

Words and Music by STEVE PERRY,
NEAL SCHON and JONATHAN CAIN

Copyright © 1981 Lacey Boulevard Music (BMI) and Weed-High Nightmare Music (BMI)
All Rights for Weed-High Nightmare Music Administered by Wixen Music Publishing Inc.
International Copyright Secured   All Rights Reserved

EDELWEISS
from THE SOUND OF MUSIC

ALTO SAX

Lyrics by OSCAR HAMMERSTEIN II
Music by RICHARD RODGERS

Copyright © 1959 by Richard Rodgers and Oscar Hammerstein II
Copyright Renewed
Williamson Music, a Division of Rodgers & Hammerstein: an Imagem Company, owner of publication and allied rights throughout the world
International Copyright Secured   All Rights Reserved

EIGHT DAYS A WEEK

ALTO SAX

Words and Music by JOHN LENNON
and PAUL McCARTNEY

Moderately fast

1., 3. Ooh, I need your love, babe; guess you know it's true.
2. Love you ev - 'ry day, girl; al - ways on my mind.

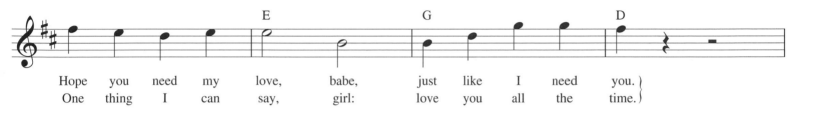

Hope you need my love, babe, just like I need you.
One thing I can say, girl: love you all the time.

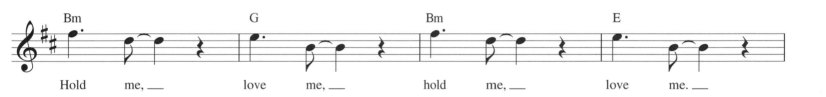

Hold me, ___ love me, ___ hold me, ___ love me. ___

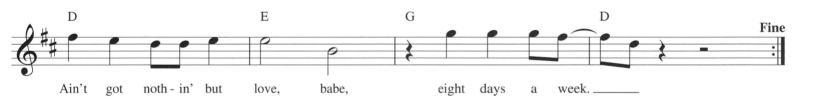

Ain't got noth - in' but love, babe, eight days a week. ___

Fine

Eight days a week I love ___ you.

Eight days a week is not e - nough to show I care. ___

D.C. al Fine

Copyright © 1964 Sony/ATV Music Publishing LLC
Copyright Renewed
All Rights Administered by Sony/ATV Music Publishing LLC, 8 Music Square West, Nashville, TN 37203
International Copyright Secured   All Rights Reserved

EVERY BREATH YOU TAKE

ALTO SAX

Music and Lyrics by
STING

© 1983 G.M. SUMNER
Administered by EMI MUSIC PUBLISHING LIMITED
All Rights Reserved   International Copyright Secured   Used by Permission

FIREFLIES

ALTO SAX

Words and Music by
ADAM YOUNG

Copyright © 2009 UNIVERSAL MUSIC CORP. and OCEAN CITY PARK
All Rights Controlled and Administered by UNIVERSAL MUSIC CORP.
All Rights Reserved   Used by Permission

GEORGIA ON MY MIND

ALTO SAX

Words by STUART GORRELL
Music by HOAGY CARMICHAEL

Copyright © 1930 by Peermusic III, Ltd.
Copyright Renewed
International Copyright Secured   All Rights Reserved

IN MY LIFE

ALTO SAX

Words and Music by JOHN LENNON
and PAUL McCARTNEY

Copyright © 1965 Sony/ATV Music Publishing LLC
Copyright Renewed
All Rights Administered by Sony/ATV Music Publishing LLC, 8 Music Square West, Nashville, TN 37203
International Copyright Secured   All Rights Reserved

HEY, SOUL SISTER

ALTO SAX

Words and Music by PAT MONAHAN,
ESPEN LIND and AMUND BJORKLAND

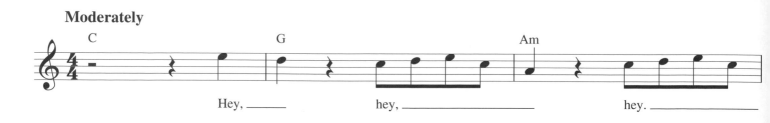

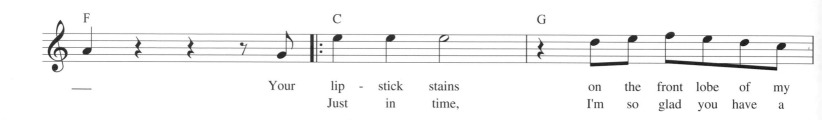

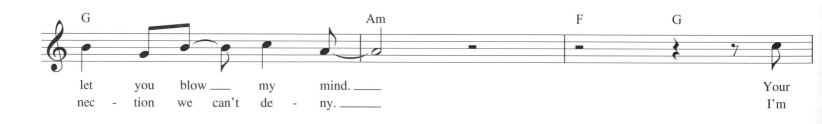

© 2009 EMI APRIL MUSIC INC., BLUE LAMP MUSIC and STELLAR SONGS LTD.
All Rights for BLUE LAMP MUSIC Controlled and Administered by EMI APRIL MUSIC INC.
All Rights for STELLAR SONGS LTD. in the U.S. and Canada Controlled and Administered by EMI BLACKWOOD MUSIC INC.
All Rights Reserved   International Copyright Secured   Used by Permission

I knew when we col - lid - ed you're the one I have de - cid - ed who's one of my kind. _
I be - lieve in you; like a vir - gin, you're Ma - don - na, and I'm al - ways gon - na

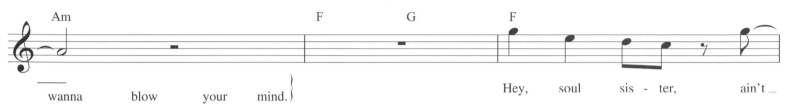

wanna blow your mind. Hey, soul sis - ter, ain't _

that Mis - ter Mis - ter on the ra - di - o, ster - e - o? The way you move ain't fair, you know.

Hey, soul sis - ter, I _ don't wan - na miss a sin - gle thing you do _

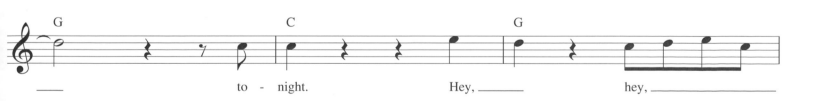

to - night. Hey, _ hey, _

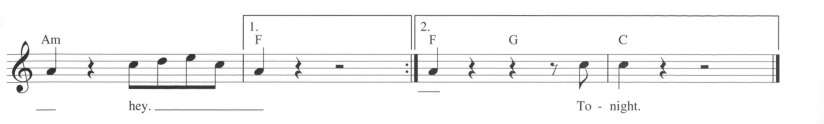

hey. _ 1. 2. To - night.

HOT N COLD

ALTO SAX

Words and Music by KATY PERRY,
MAX MARTIN and LUKASZ GOTTWALD

Moderately fast

You change your mind ___ like a girl ___ chang-es clothes. ___
We used to be ___ just like twins, ___ so in sync. ___

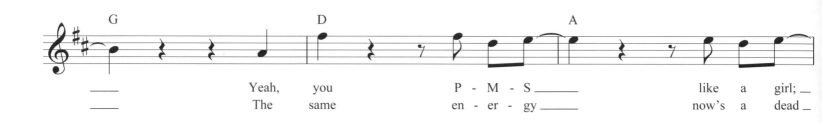

___ Yeah, you P - M - S ___ like a girl; ___
___ The same en - er - gy ___ now's a dead ___

___ I would know. ___ And you o - ver - think, ___
___ bat - ter - y. ___ Used to laugh 'bout noth - ing; ___

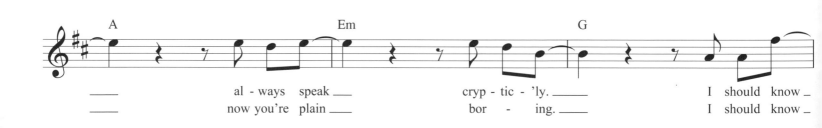

___ al - ways speak ___ cryp - tic - 'ly. ___ I should know _
___ now you're plain ___ bor - ing. ___ I should know _

___ that you're ___ no good ___ for me. ___
___ that you're ___ not gon - na change. ___

© 2008 WHEN I'M RICH YOU'LL BE MY BITCH, MARATONE AB, KASZ MONEY PUBLISHING and PRESCRIPTION SONGS
All Rights for WHEN I'M RICH YOU'LL BE MY BITCH Administered by WB MUSIC CORP.
All Rights for MARATONE AB, KASZ MONEY PUBLISHING and PRESCRIPTION SONGS Administered by KOBALT MUSIC PUBLISHING AMERICA, INC.
All Rights Reserved   Used by Permission

'Cause you're hot ____ then you're cold. You're yes ____ then you're no. You're in ____

____ then you're out. You're up ____ then you're down. You're wrong ____ when it's right. It's black ____

____ and it's white. We fight, ____ we break up. We kiss, ____ we make up. ____

You don't real - ly wan - na stay, no, ____ but you don't real - ly wan - na

go. _____ You're hot ____ then you're cold. You're yes ____ then you're no. You're in ____

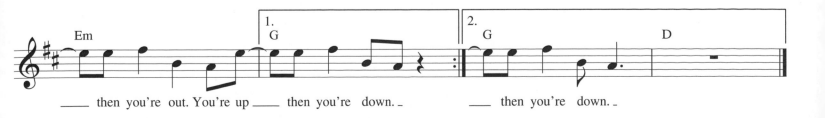

____ then you're out. You're up ____ then you're down. ____   ____ then you're down. ____

ISN'T SHE LOVELY

ALTO SAX

Words and Music by
STEVIE WONDER

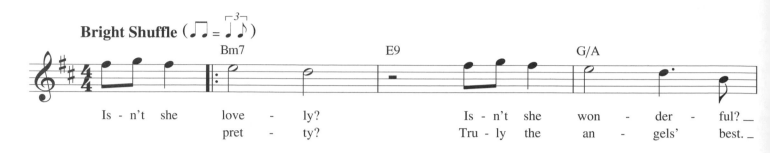

Bright Shuffle

Is - n't she love - ly?
pret - ty?

Is - n't she won - der - ful? ___
Tru - ly the an - gels' best. ___

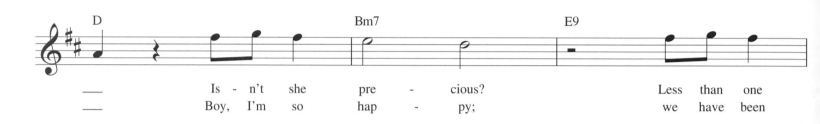

___ Is - n't she pre - cious?
___ Boy, I'm so hap - py;

Less than one
we have been

min - ute old. _____
heav - en blessed. ___

I nev - er thought ___
I can't be - lieve _____

through love we'd be ___
what God has done. ___

___
___

mak - ing one as love - ly _____ as she. ___
Through us He's giv - en life ___ to one. ___

But is - n't she

love - ly? Made from love.

1.
Is - n't she

2.

© 1976 (Renewed 2004) JOBETE MUSIC CO., INC. and BLACK BULL MUSIC
c/o EMI APRIL MUSIC INC.
All Rights Reserved International Copyright Secured Used by Permission

THE LETTER

ALTO SAX

Words and Music by
WAYNE CARSON THOMPSON

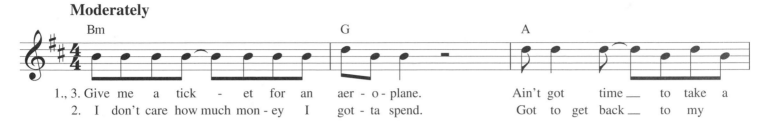

Moderately

1., 3. Give me a tick - et for an aer - o - plane. Ain't got time __ to take a
2. I don't care how much mon - ey I got - ta spend. Got to get back __ to my

fast __ train. } Lone - ly days are gone; __ I'm a - go - in' home. __ Oh, my
ba - by again. }

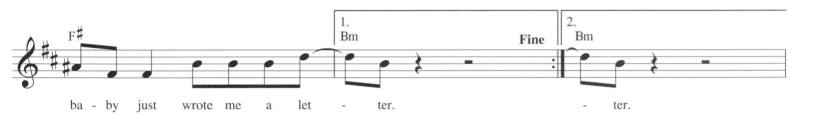

ba - by just wrote me a let - ter. - ter.

1. Bm **Fine** | **2.** Bm

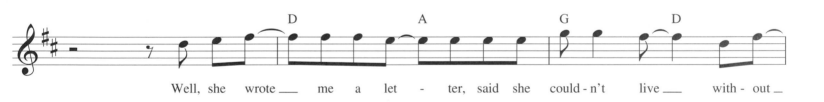

Well, she wrote __ me a let - ter, said she could - n't live __ with - out __

__ me no more. Lis - ten, mis - ter, can't you see I

D.C. al Fine
(take 1st ending)

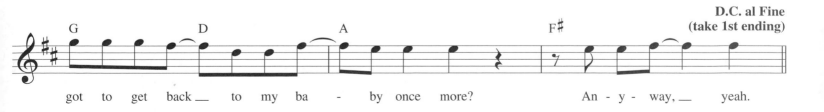

got to get back __ to my ba - by once more? An - y - way, __ yeah.

© 1967 (Renewed) Budde Songs, Inc. and Lovolar Music
All Rights Administered by Bike Music c/o The Bicycle Music Company
All Rights Reserved   Used by Permission

LIKE A VIRGIN

ALTO SAX

Words and Music by BILLY STEINBERG
and TOM KELLY

Copyright © 1984 Sony/ATV Music Publishing LLC
All Rights Administered by Sony/ATV Music Publishing LLC, 8 Music Square West, Nashville, TN 37203
International Copyright Secured   All Rights Reserved

THE LOOK OF LOVE

from *CASINO ROYALE*

ALTO SAX

Words by HAL DAVID
Music by BURT BACHARACH

© 1967 (Renewed 1995) COLGEMS-EMI MUSIC INC.
All Rights Reserved International Copyright Secured Used by Permission

LOVE ME TENDER

ALTO SAX

Words and Music by ELVIS PRESLEY
and VERA MATSON

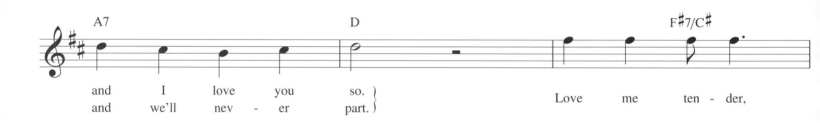

Copyright © 1956; Renewed 1984 Elvis Presley Music (BMI)
All Rights in the U.S. Administered by Imagem Sounds
International Copyright Secured   All Rights Reserved

MR. TAMBOURINE MAN

ALTO SAX

Words and Music by
BOB DYLAN

Copyright © 1964, 1965 Warner Bros. Inc.
Copyright Renewed 1992, 1996 Special Rider Music
International Copyright Secured   All Rights Reserved
Reprinted by Permission of Music Sales Corporation

LOVE STORY

ALTO SAX

Words and Music by
TAYLOR SWIFT

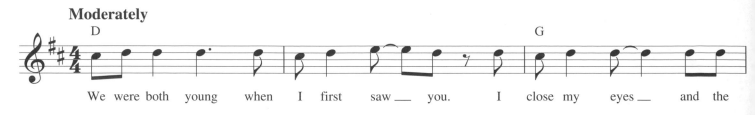

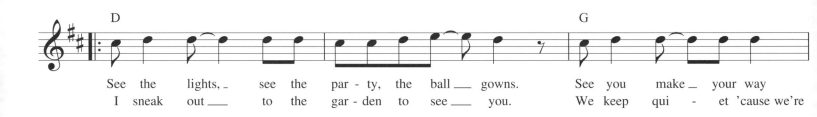

Copyright © 2008 Sony/ATV Music Publishing LLC and Taylor Swift Music
All Rights Administered by Sony/ATV Music Publishing LLC, 8 Music Square West, Nashville, TN 37203
International Copyright Secured   All Rights Reserved

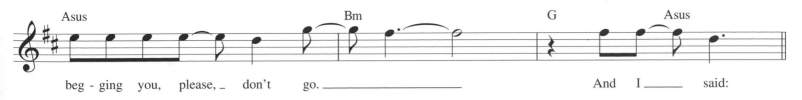

beg - ging you, please, _ don't go. _____ And I _____ said:

Ro - me - o, take me some-where we can be a - lone. I'll be wait - ing.

All there's left to do is run. You'll be the prince and I'll be the prin - cess.

It's a love sto - ry. __ Ba - by, just say yes. So

Ba - by, just say __ yes. _____ Oh, __ oh, oh. __

Oh, __ oh, oh, _____ oh.

'Cause we were both young when I first saw __ you. __

MOON RIVER

from the Paramount Picture BREAKFAST AT TIFFANY'S

ALTO SAX

Words by JOHNNY MERCER
Music by HENRY MANCINI

Copyright © 1961 Sony/ATV Music Publishing LLC
Copyright Renewed
All Rights Administered by Sony/ATV Music Publishing LLC, 8 Music Square West, Nashville, TN 37203
International Copyright Secured   All Rights Reserved

MORNING HAS BROKEN

ALTO SAX

Words by ELEANOR FARJEON
Music by CAT STEVENS

Copyright © 1971 Cat Music Ltd. and BMG Rights Management (UK) Ltd., a BMG Chrysalis company
Copyright Renewed
All Rights Reserved Used by Permission

MY CHERIE AMOUR

ALTO SAX

Words and Music by STEVIE WONDER,
SYLVIA MOY and HENRY COSBY

© 1968 (Renewed 1996) JOBETE MUSIC CO., INC., BLACK BULL MUSIC and SAWANDI MUSIC
c/o EMI APRIL MUSIC INC. and EMI BLACKWOOD MUSIC INC.
All Rights Reserved International Copyright Secured Used by Permission

MY GIRL

ALTO SAX

Words and Music by WILLIAM "SMOKEY" ROBINSON
and RONALD WHITE

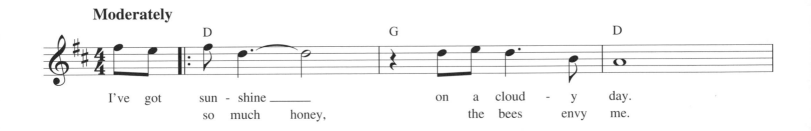

I've got sun - shine _____ on a cloud - y day.
so much honey, the bees envy me.

When it's cold out - side, I've got the month of
I've got a sweet - er song than the birds in the

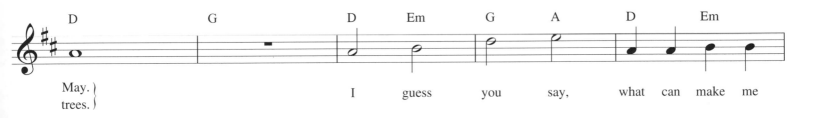

May.
trees. I guess you say, what can make me

feel this way? My girl. (My girl, my girl.) Talk - in' 'bout

my girl. _____ (My girl.) I've got (My girl.)

© 1964, 1972, 1973, 1977 (Renewed 1992, 2000, 2001, 2005) JOBETE MUSIC CO., INC.
All Rights Controlled and Administered by EMI APRIL MUSIC INC.
All Rights Reserved   International Copyright Secured   Used by Permission

MY FAVORITE THINGS

from THE SOUND OF MUSIC

ALTO SAX

Lyrics by OSCAR HAMMERSTEIN II
Music by RICHARD RODGERS

Copyright © 1959 by Richard Rodgers and Oscar Hammerstein II
Copyright Renewed
Williamson Music, a Division of Rodgers & Hammerstein: an Imagem Company, owner of publication and allied rights throughout the world
International Copyright Secured   All Rights Reserved

MY HEART WILL GO ON

(Love Theme from 'Titanic')

from the Paramount and Twentieth Century Fox Motion Picture TITANIC

ALTO SAX

Music by JAMES HORNER
Lyric by WILL JENNINGS

Copyright © 1997 Sony/ATV Music Publishing LLC, T C F Music Publishing, Inc., Fox Film Music Corporation and Blue Sky Rider Songs
All Rights on behalf of Sony/ATV Music Publishing LLC Administered by Sony/ATV Music Publishing LLC, 8 Music Square West, Nashville, TN 37203
All Rights on behalf of Blue Sky Rider Songs Administered by Irving Music, Inc.
International Copyright Secured   All Rights Reserved

NIGHTS IN WHITE SATIN

ALTO SAX

Words and Music by
JUSTIN HAYWARD

Moderately fast

Am

G

Am

Nights in white sat - in, _____ nev - er reach - ing the
Gaz - ing at peo - ple, _____ some hand in

G

F

C

end. _____
hand. _____

Let - ters I've writ - ten, _____
Just what I'm go - ing through,

Bb

Am

nev - er mean - ing to send. _____ Beau - ty I'd
they _ can't un - der - stand. _____ Some try to

G

Am

G

al - ways missed with these eyes _ be - fore. _____
tell me _____ thoughts they can-not de - fend. _____

F

C

Bb

Just what the truth is, _____ I can't say an - y -
Just what you want to be, you'll be in the

Am

D

more. _____ 'Cause I } love you, _____ yes, I ____
end. _____ And I }

F

Am

love you. _____ Oh, _____ how __ I love __ you. _____

G

Am

1.
G

2.

© Copyright 1967 (Renewed), 1968 (Renewed) and 1970 (Renewed) Tyler Music Ltd., London, England
TRO - Essex Music, Inc., New York, controls all publication rights for the U.S.A. and Canada
International Copyright Secured
All Rights Reserved Including Public Performance For Profit
Used by Permission

NOWHERE MAN

ALTO SAX

Words and Music by JOHN LENNON and PAUL McCARTNEY

Copyright © 1965 Sony/ATV Music Publishing LLC
Copyright Renewed
All Rights Administered by Sony/ATV Music Publishing LLC, 8 Music Square West, Nashville, TN 37203
International Copyright Secured   All Rights Reserved

PUFF THE MAGIC DRAGON

ALTO SAX

Words and Music by LENNY LIPTON
and PETER YARROW

Copyright © 1963; Renewed 1991 Honalee Melodies (ASCAP) and Silver Dawn Music (ASCAP)
Worldwide Rights for Honalee Melodies Administered by BMG Rights Management (US) LLC
Worldwide Rights for Silver Dawn Music Administered by WB Music Corp.
International Copyright Secured   All Rights Reserved

RAINDROPS KEEP FALLIN' ON MY HEAD
from BUTCH CASSIDY AND THE SUNDANCE KID

ALTO SAX

Lyric by HAL DAVID
Music by BURT BACHARACH

Copyright © 1969 (Renewed) Casa David, New Hidden Valley Music and WB Music Corp.
International Copyright Secured   All Rights Reserved

SCARBOROUGH FAIR/CANTICLE

ALTO SAX

Arrangement and Original Counter Melody by PAUL SIMON
and ARTHUR GARFUNKEL

Copyright © 1966 (Renewed) Paul Simon and Arthur Garfunkel (BMI)
International Copyright Secured   All Rights Reserved
Used by Permission

SOMEWHERE OUT THERE
from AN AMERICAN TAIL

ALTO SAX

Music by BARRY MANN and JAMES HORNER
Lyric by CYNTHIA WEIL

Moderately

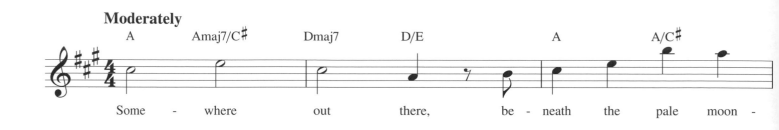

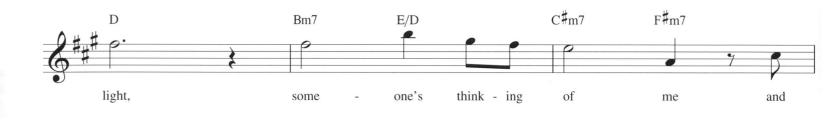

Some - where   out   there,   be - neath   the   pale   moon - light,

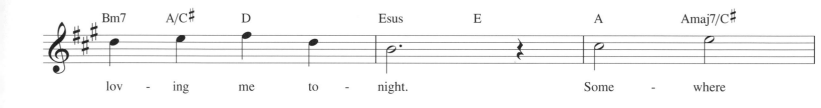

some - one's   think - ing   of   me   and   lov - ing   me   to - night.   Some - where

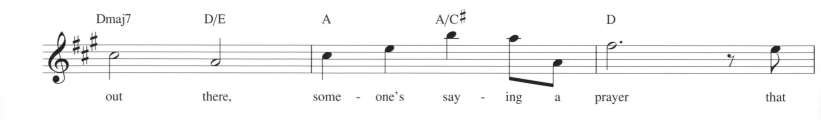

out   there,   some - one's   say - ing   a   prayer   that

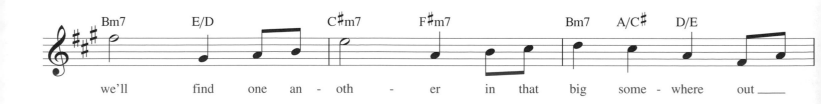

we'll   find   one   an - oth - er   in   that   big   some - where   out ___

Copyright © 1986 USI A MUSIC PUBLISHING and USI B MUSIC PUBLISHING
All Rights Controlled and Administered by UNIVERSAL MUSIC CORP. and SONGS OF UNIVERSAL, INC.
All Rights Reserved   Used by Permission

there.   And e - ven though I know how ver - y far a - part we are,   it

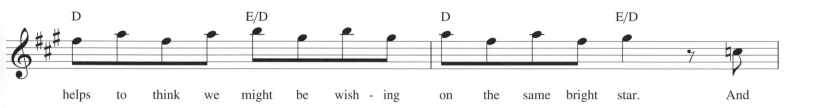

helps to think we might be wish - ing on the same bright star.   And

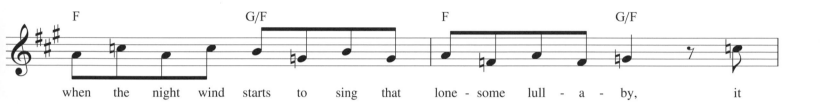

when the night wind starts to sing that lone - some lull - a - by,   it

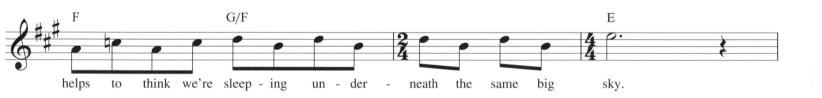

helps to think we're sleep - ing un - der - neath the same big sky.

Some - where   out there,   if love can see us

through,   then we'll be to - geth - er some - where

out there,   out where dreams come true.

THE SOUND OF MUSIC
from THE SOUND OF MUSIC

ALTO SAX

Lyrics by OSCAR HAMMERSTEIN II
Music by RICHARD RODGERS

Moderately

The hills are a-live with the sound of mu - sic, _____ with

songs they have sung for a thou-sand years. _____ The

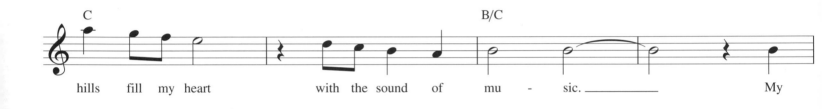

hills fill my heart with the sound of mu - sic. _____ My

heart wants to sing ev-'ry song it hears. _____ My heart wants to

beat like the wings of the birds that rise from the lake to the

trees. My heart wants to sigh like a chime that flies from a

Copyright © 1959 by Richard Rodgers and Oscar Hammerstein II
Copyright Renewed
Williamson Music, a Division of Rodgers & Hammerstein: an Imagem Company, owner of publication and allied rights throughout the world
International Copyright Secured   All Rights Reserved

47

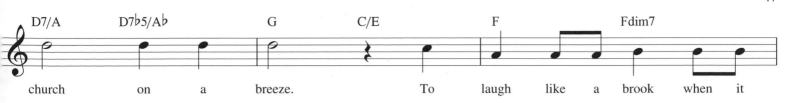

church   on   a   breeze.   To   laugh   like   a   brook   when   it

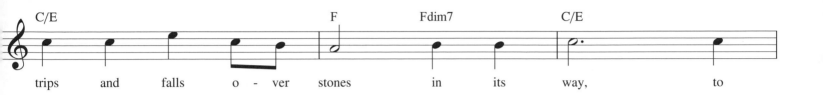

trips   and   falls   o - ver   stones   in   its   way,   to

sing   through   the   night   like   a   lark   who   is   learn - ing   to   pray.   I

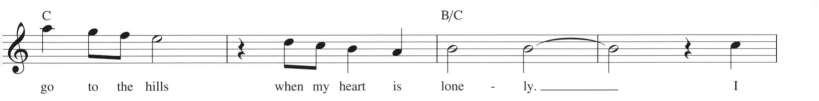

go   to   the   hills   when   my   heart   is   lone - ly. _____   I

know   I   will   hear   what   I've   heard   be - fore. _____   My

heart   will   be   blessed   with   the   sound   of   mu - sic, _____   and   I'll

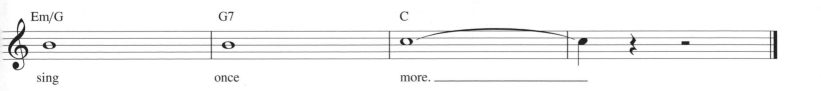

sing   once   more. _____

STRANGERS IN THE NIGHT
adapted from A MAN COULD GET KILLED

Alto Sax

Words by CHARLES SINGLETON and EDDIE SNYDER
Music by BERT KAEMPFERT

Copyright © 1966 SONGS OF UNIVERSAL, INC. and SCREEN GEMS-EMI MUSIC INC.
Copyright Renewed
All Rights for the World Controlled and Administered by SONGS OF UNIVERSAL, INC.
All Rights Reserved   Used by Permission

SUNSHINE ON MY SHOULDERS

Alto Sax

Words by JOHN DENVER
Music by JOHN DENVER, MIKE TAYLOR
and DICK KNISS

Copyright © 1971; Renewed 1999 BMG Ruby Songs, Anna Kate Deutschendorf,
Zachary Deutschendorf, BMG Rights Management (Ireland) Ltd. and Jesse Belle Denver in the U.S.
All Rights for BMG Ruby Songs, Anna Kate Deutschendorf and Zachary Deutschendorf Administered by BMG Rights Management (US) LLC
All Rights for BMG Rights Management (Ireland) Ltd. Administered by Chrysalis One Music
All Rights for Jesse Belle Denver Administered by WB Music Corp.
International Copyright Secured   All Rights Reserved

SWEET CAROLINE

ALTO SAX

Words and Music by
NEIL DIAMOND

Moderately

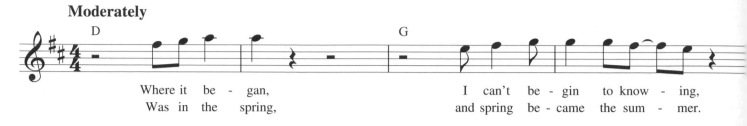

Where it be - gan, I can't be - gin to know - ing,
Was in the spring, and spring be - came the sum - mer.

but then, I know it's grow - ing strong.
Who'd have be - lieved you'd come _ a -

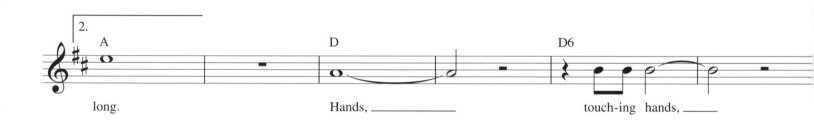

long. Hands, _____ touch-ing hands, _____

reach-ing out, touch-ing me, touch-ing you. _____

Sweet Car - o - line, _____ good times nev - er seemed so
I've been in - clined _____ to be - lieve they nev - er

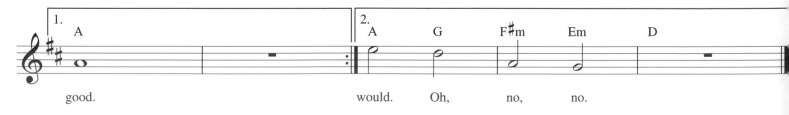

good. would. Oh, no, no.

Copyright © 1969 Stonebridge Music
Copyright Renewed
All Rights Administered by Sony/ATV Music Publishing LLC, 8 Music Square West, Nashville, TN 37203
International Copyright Secured   All Rights Reserved

TILL THERE WAS YOU

from Meredith Willson's THE MUSIC MAN

ALTO SAX

By MEREDITH WILLSON

© 1950, 1957 (Renewed) FRANK MUSIC CORP. and MEREDITH WILLSON MUSIC
All Rights Reserved

THE TIMES THEY ARE A-CHANGIN'

ALTO SAX

Words and Music by
BOB DYLAN

Copyright © 1963 Warner Bros. Inc.
Copyright Renewed 1991 Special Rider Music
International Copyright Secured   All Rights Reserved
Reprinted by Permission of Music Sales Corporation

UNCHAINED MELODY

ALTO SAX

Lyric by HY ZARET
Music by ALEX NORTH

© 1955 (Renewed) North Ohana Publishing (ASCAP) and HZUM Publishing (ASCAP)
c/o Unchained Melody Publishing, LLC
All Rights Reserved   Used by Permission

TOMORROW
from The Musical Production ANNIE

ALTO SAX

Lyric by MARTIN CHARNIN
Music by CHARLES STROUSE

Moderately fast

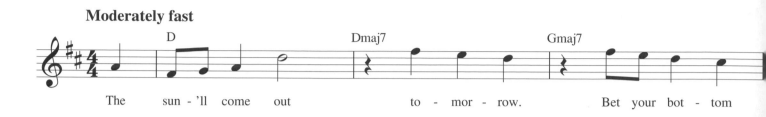

The sun - 'll come out to - mor - row. Bet your bot - tom

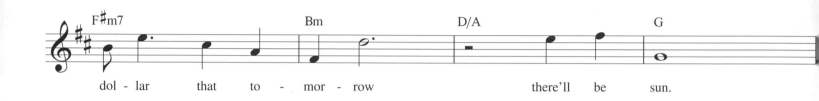

dol - lar that to - mor - row there'll be sun.

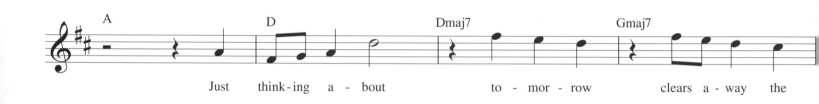

Just think - ing a - bout to - mor - row clears a - way the

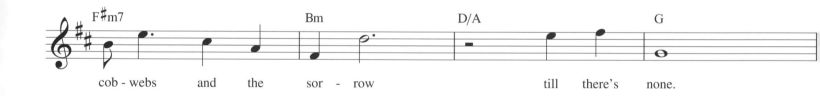

cob - webs and the sor - row till there's none.

When I'm stuck with a day that's gray and lone - ly,

I just stick out my chin and grin and say, _____

© 1977 (Renewed) EDWIN H. MORRIS & COMPANY, A Division of MPL Music Publishing, Inc. and CHARLES STROUSE
All rights on behalf of CHARLES STROUSE owned by CHARLES STROUSE PUBLISHING (Administered by WILLIAMSON MUSIC,
a Division of Rodgers & Hammerstein: an Imagem Company)
All Rights Reserved   Used by Permission
www.CharlesStrouse.com

oh: _____ The sun - 'll come out

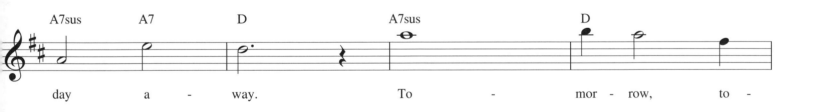

to - mor - row, so you got - ta hang on till to - mor - row,

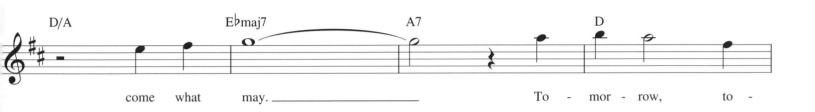

come what may. _____ To - mor - row, to -

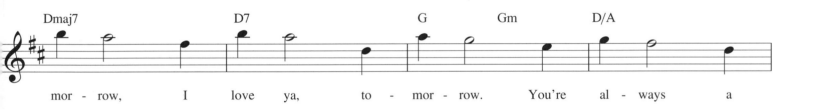

mor - row, I love ya, to - mor - row. You're al - ways a

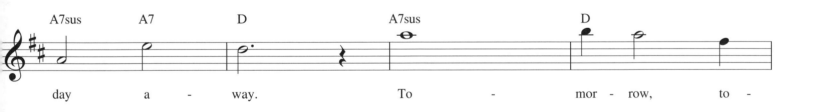

day a - way. To - mor - row, to -

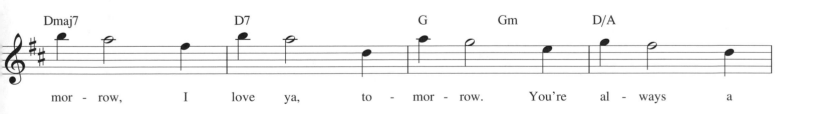

mor - row, I love ya, to - mor - row. You're al - ways a

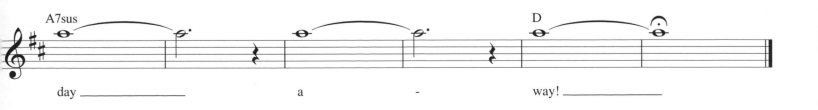

day _____ a - way! _____

VIVA LA VIDA

ALTO SAX

Words and Music by GUY BERRYMAN,
JON BUCKLAND, WILL CHAMPION
and CHRIS MARTIN

Moderately

I used to rule the world. ___ Seas would rise when I gave the word. ___

___ Now in the morn - ing I sleep a - lone, ___ sweep the

streets I used to own. ___

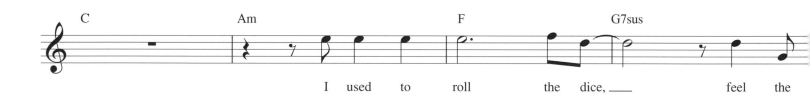

I used to roll the dice, ___ feel the

fear in my en - e - my's eyes, ___ lis - ten as the crowd ___ would sing, ___

___ "Now the old king is dead; ___ long live the king." One min - ute I

held the key, ___ next the walls were closed on

Copyright © 2008 by Universal Music Publishing MGB Ltd.
All Rights in the United States and Canada Administered by Universal Music - MGB Songs
International Copyright Secured All Rights Reserved

me. And I dis-cov-ered that my cas - tles stand ____ up - on

pil-lars of salt ____ and pil-lars of sand. ____ I hear Je - ru - sa - lem bells __

____ a - ring - ing. Ro - man cav - al - ry choirs ____ are sing - ing.

Be my mir-ror, my sword ____ and shield, ____ my mis-sion-ar - ies in a for -

- eign field. ____ For some rea - son I can't ____ ex - plain, __

once you've gone there was nev - er, nev - er an hon - est word, __

____ and that was when I ruled the world. __

WE ARE THE WORLD

ALTO SAX

Words and Music by LIONEL RICHIE
and MICHAEL JACKSON

Moderately

C   F/C   G/C   C

There comes a time ___ when we heed a cer - tain call, ___ when the
We can't go on ___ pre - tend - ing day ___ by day ___ that some-

F   G   C

world must come to - geth - er as one. There are peo -
one some - where will soon make a change. We are all ___

Am   Em7

- ple dy - ing, oh, and it's time ___ to lend a hand to life,
___ a part ___ of God's ___ great ___ big fam - i - ly, and the

Dm7   F

1. Gsus   G

2. Gsus

the great - est gift ___ of all. ___
truth, you know love is all ___ we need. ___

G   F   G   C

___ We are the world, ___ we are the chil - dren.

F   G   C

We are the ones ___ who make a bright - er day, ___ so let's ___ start giv - ing.

Am   Em7

There's a choice we're mak - ing; ___ we're sav - ing our ___ own lives.

Dm7   G7sus   C

___ It's true: ___ we make a bet - ter day, ___ just you ___ and me. ___

Copyright © 1985 by Brockman Music, Brenda Richie Publishing, Warner-Tamerlane Publishing Corp. and Mijac Music
All Rights on behalf of Mijac Music Administered by Sony/ATV Music Publishing LLC, 8 Music Square West, Nashville, TN 37203
All Rights Reserved Used by Permission

WHAT A WONDERFUL WORLD

Alto Sax

Words and Music by GEORGE DAVID WEISS
and BOB THIELE

Copyright © 1967 by Range Road Music Inc., Quartet Music and Abilene Music, Inc.
Copyright Renewed
All Rights for Quartet Music Administered by BUG Music, Inc., a BMG Chrysalis company
All Rights for Abilene Music, Inc. Administered Worldwide by Imagem Music LLC
International Copyright Secured   All Rights Reserved
Used by Permission

WONDERWALL

ALTO SAX

Words and Music by
NOEL GALLAGHER

Copyright © 1995 SM Music Publishing UK Limited and Oasis Music
All Rights Administered by Sony/ATV Music Publishing LLC, 8 Music Square West, Nashville, TN 37203
International Copyright Secured   All Rights Reserved

61

the lights that lead us there are blind - ing.

There are man - y things that I would like to say to you, _

but I don't know how. _____

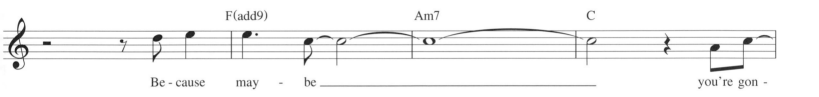

Be - cause may - be _____ you're gon -

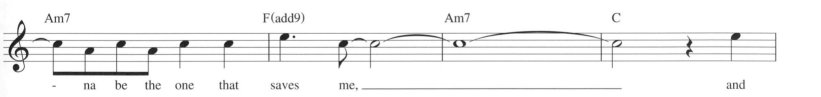

- na be the one that saves me, _____ and

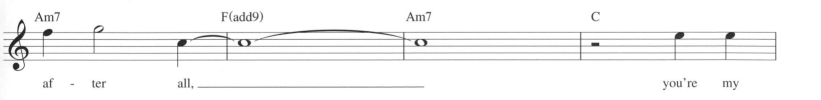

af - ter all, _____ you're my

won - der - wall. _____

YOU ARE THE SUNSHINE OF MY LIFE

ALTO SAX

Words and Music by
STEVIE WONDER

Brightly

You are the sun - shine of _ my life. _
You are the ap - ple of _ my eye. _

That's why I'll al - ways be _ a - round. _
For - ev - er you'll _ stay in _ my heart. _

I feel like this _ is the _ be - gin - ning, _

though I've loved you _ for a thou - sand years. _

And if I thought _ our love _ was end - ing, _ I'd find _

D.C. al Fine
(take repeat)

_ my - self _ drown - ing in my _ own tears. Whoa, _ whoa. _

© 1972 (Renewed 2000) JOBETE MUSIC CO., INC. and BLACK BULL MUSIC
c/o EMI APRIL MUSIC INC.
All Rights Reserved   International Copyright Secured   Used by Permission

YOU'VE GOT A FRIEND

ALTO SAX

Words and Music by
CAROLE KING

© 1971 (Renewed 1999) COLGEMS-EMI MUSIC INC.
All Rights Reserved   International Copyright Secured   Used by Permission

Audio Access Included

HAL•LEONARD
EASY INSTRUMENTAL PLAY-ALONG

- Perfect for beginning players
- Carefully edited to include only the notes and rhythms that students learn in the first months playing their instrument

- Great-sounding demonstration and play-along tracks
- Audio tracks can be accessed online for download or streaming, using the unique code inside the book

DISNEY
Book with Online Audio Tracks

The Ballad of Davy Crockett • Can You Feel the Love Tonight • Candle on the Water • I Just Can't Wait to Be King • The Medallion Calls • Mickey Mouse March • Part of Your World • Whistle While You Work • You Can Fly! You Can Fly! You Can Fly! • You'll Be in My Heart (Pop Version).

00122184	Flute	$9.99
00122185	Clarinet	$9.99
00122186	Alto Sax	$9.99
00122187	Tenor Sax	$9.99
00122188	Trumpet	$9.99
00122189	Horn	$9.99
00122190	Trombone	$9.99
00122191	Violin	$9.99
00122192	Viola	$9.99
00122193	Cello	$9.99
00122194	Keyboard Percussion	$9.99

CLASSIC ROCK
Book with Online Audio Tracks

Another One Bites the Dust • Born to Be Wild • Brown Eyed Girl • Dust in the Wind • Every Breath You Take • Fly like an Eagle • I Heard It Through the Grapevine • I Shot the Sheriff • Oye Como Va • Up Around the Bend.

00122195	Flute	$9.99
00122196	Clarinet	$9.99
00122197	Alto Sax	$9.99
00122198	Tenor Sax	$9.99
00122201	Trumpet	$9.99
00122202	Horn	$9.99
00122203	Trombone	$9.99
00122205	Violin	$9.99
00122206	Viola	$9.99
00122207	Cello	$9.99
00122208	Keyboard Percussion	$9.99

CLASSICAL THEMES
Book with Online Audio Tracks

Can Can • Carnival of Venice • Finlandia • Largo from Symphony No. 9 ("New World") • Morning • Musette in D Major • Ode to Joy • Spring • Symphony No. 1 in C Minor, Fourth Movement Excerpt • Trumpet Voluntary.

00123108	Flute	$9.99
00123109	Clarinet	$9.99
00123110	Alto Sax	$9.99
00123111	Tenor Sax	$9.99
00123112	Trumpet	$9.99
00123113	Horn	$9.99
00123114	Trombone	$9.99
00123115	Violin	$9.99
00123116	Viola	$9.99
00123117	Cello	$9.99
00123118	Keyboard Percussion	$9.99

CHRISTMAS CAROLS
Book with Online Audio Tracks

Angels We Have Heard on High • Christ Was Born on Christmas Day • Come, All Ye Shepherds • Come, Thou Long-Expected Jesus • Good Christian Men, Rejoice • Jingle Bells • Jolly Old St. Nicholas • Lo, How a Rose E'er Blooming • On Christmas Night • Up on the Housetop.

00130363	Flute	$9.99
00130364	Clarinet	$9.99
00130365	Alto Sax	$9.99
00130366	Tenor Sax	$9.99
00130367	Trumpet	$9.99
00130368	Horn	$9.99
00130369	Trombone	$9.99
00130370	Violin	$9.99
00130371	Viola	$9.99
00130372	Cello	$9.99
00130373	Keyboard Percussion	$9.99

POP FAVORITES
Book with Online Audio Tracks

Achy Breaky Heart (Don't Tell My Heart) • I'm a Believer • Imagine • Jailhouse Rock • La Bamba • Louie, Louie • Ob-La-Di, Ob-La-Da • Splish Splash • Stand by Me • Yellow Submarine.

00232231	Flute	$9.99
00232232	Clarinet	$9.99
00232233	Alto Sax	$9.99
00232234	Tenor Sax	$9.99
00232235	Trumpet	$9.99
00232236	Horn	$9.99
00232237	Trombone	$9.99
00232238	Violin	$9.99
00232239	Viola	$9.99
00232240	Cello	$9.99
00233296	Keyboard Percussion	$9.99

Disney characters and artwork © Disney Enterprises, Inc.

HAL•LEONARD®

www.halleonard.com

Prices, content, and availability subject to change without notice.